Pollution

Janine Amos

Watts Books
London • New York • Sydney

© Watts Books 1992
Paperback edition 1995

Watts Books
96 Leonard Street
London EC2A 4RH

Franklin Watts Australia
14 Mars Road
Lane Cove
NSW 2066

ISBN: 0 7496 0711 4 (hardback)
ISBN: 0 7496 2323 3 (paperback)

10 9 8 7 6 5 4 3 2 1

Editor: Ambreen Husain
Designer: Shaun Barlow
Cover Design: K and Co
Artwork: Brian McIntyre
Cover Artwork: Hayward Art Group
Picture Research: Ambreen Husain

Educational Advisor: Joy Richardson

A CIP catalogue record for this book
is available from the British Library

Printed in Italy
by G. Canale & Co. SpA

Contents

What does pollution mean?

Wherever we live in the world we need clean air to breathe and clean water to drink. We need safe healthy soil in which to grow food crops. Our world provides all these things but they are being spoiled by large amounts of **waste** and other harmful substances. This is called **pollution**. There are many different kinds of pollution.

▽ Litter is one kind of pollution. Crowds of people often leave lots of litter behind.

A dirty world

The pollution of air, water and soil are all linked. Smoke pollutes the air, but rain carries the dirt into water and soil too. And winds blow pollution from the land into rivers and seas. By polluting one part of the world, we can harm another part. Most of the pollution in the world is the result of human activity. The number of people in the world is increasing all the time, adding to pollution problems.

▷ Canals and rivers are often polluted by rubbish.

▽ Pollution gets carried by the wind. Rubbish is also blown about.

▷ Factory smoke and car fumes pollute the air.

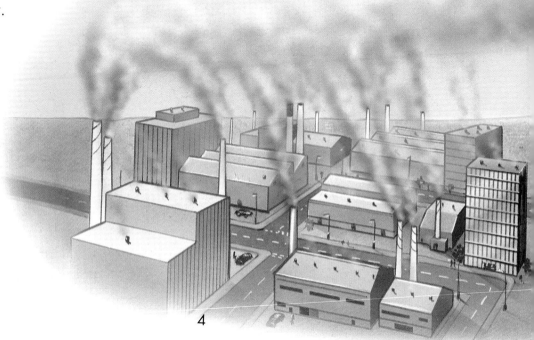

◁ Rain carries pollution into water and soil.

Dirty air

Some power stations burn **fuels** like coal, oil and gas to produce electricity. Cars, trains, ships and aeroplanes burn petrol and diesel fuel for power. As these fuels burn they produce harmful waste gases. Factories also pollute the air. It is easy to see clouds of smoke polluting the air, but pollution can be invisible. Not all pollution is man-made. Volcanoes can produce huge clouds of dust and gas.

▷ Volcanoes produce a gas called sulphur dioxide. This can be harmful in large amounts.

▷ Clouds of smoke from factories pollute the air.

▽ Pollution from traffic hangs over this city. It is called smog.

Acid rain

When smoke and gases from factories and cars mix with water in the air this makes acid. The acid is carried by the wind in clouds, sometimes for thousands of kilometres. When rain falls from the clouds, the acid falls to earth. This is called **acid rain**. It harms buildings. It kills trees. When acid rain falls on lakes and rivers, the water becomes acidic. Fish and water plants cannot survive in it.

▷ Acid rain is wearing away important stone buildings.

▽ Acid rain attacks trees through their leaves and through the soil. Whole forests are dying.

Getting warmer

The earth is kept warm by the sun's heat. Gases in the **atmosphere** around the earth keep in some of the heat. This is called the **greenhouse effect**, because the gases stop some of the heat escaping, just like the glass of a greenhouse. Pollution is putting more gases that trap heat into the atmosphere. This is causing our world to warm up. A warmer world would bring changes. Sea levels may rise, causing cities to be flooded.

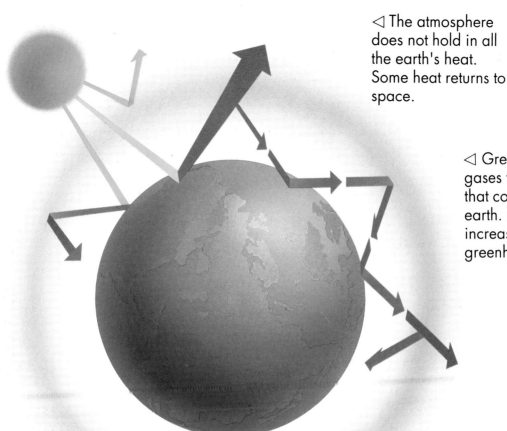

◁ The atmosphere does not hold in all the earth's heat. Some heat returns to space.

◁ Greenhouse gases trap the heat that comes from the earth. Pollution is increasing this greenhouse effect.

▷ Chemicals called CFCs are used in fridges and aerosols. They can trap large amounts of heat when they are released into the atmosphere.

◁ People are burning rainforests to make space for farms. The fires produce gases which make the atmosphere warm up.

Dirty water

Some factories and cities use rivers to get rid of their waste. All kinds of poisons are pumped into rivers and carried downstream. Some build up to dangerous levels in the bodies of fish and birds. Other kinds of pollution speed up the growth of some water plants. They make the water dark and smelly. It becomes difficult for other wildlife to live in it.

▽ Factory waste has threatened the life of Lake Baikal in Siberia.

◁ This pipe belongs to a factory. It pours waste water and poisons straight into a river.

▷ Some detergents end up in rivers. They can cause tiny plants to grow so quickly that they take over the river.

◁ In polluted water fish choke to death or die because of poisons.

Polluting the sea

Rivers drain into the sea. They carry the pollution with them. Waste from seaside homes and factories is often pumped straight into the ocean. Sea animals are poisoned. People eating them become ill.

The sea is used as a giant dustbin. As the world's population increases, the amount of waste dumped into the sea increases.

▷ Dirty water from sinks and toilets pours straight into the sea from this pipe.

◁ The mussels on this mussel farm may be poisoned by pollution in the sea.

▷ Some of the waste
dumped into oceans
will stay dangerous
for hundreds of
years.

Oil pollution

Our seas are polluted by oil too. Oil tankers carry thousands of tonnes of oil. Accidents cause oil spills. Some oil tankers wash out their tanks with sea water. There are also leaks from pipelines under the sea.

Spilled oil floats on the water in huge **slicks** and washes on to beaches in thick black lumps. Many sea creatures swallow the oil or become coated in it.

▷ These people are cleaning the sticky oil off a bird's feathers.

◁ Tanker accidents cause oil spills. Animals like this seal are harmed and can die.

▷ Oil from spills drifts onto beaches, spoiling them for wildlife and people.

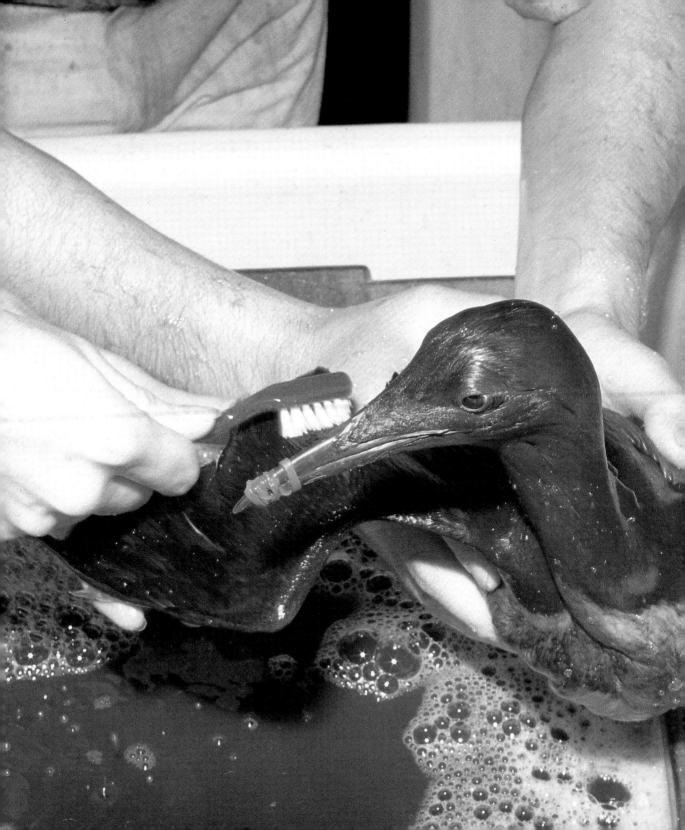

Spoiling the soil

Farms produce the crops we eat as food. But many farms cause pollution. Chemical **fertilizers** help crops grow, but too much fertilizer harms the soil. Crops are sprayed with **pesticides** to kill insect pests, but the sprays may poison harmless animals. People may be poisoned too. Rain washes pesticides and fertilizers from the soil into rivers, polluting the water with harmful chemicals.

▷ Pesticides sprayed on crops travel through the air and can poison wildlife.

▷ Farmers use poisonous sprays to kill crop-eating insects. But much of the spray never reaches the pests.

spray drifts onto grass in fields

∨ Pesticides reach people through food. Scientists do not yet know how dangerous this is.

sprayed wheat

rain washes spray into rivers

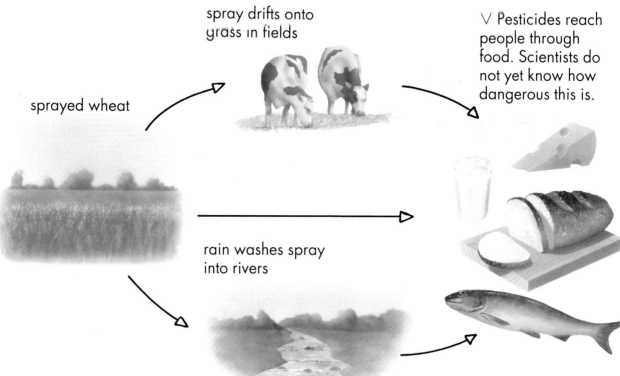

Accidents

Even small amounts of pollution can make people ill. Dirty air can make our eyes burn and our chests hurt. Dirty water can spread many diseases. A factory accident may mean disaster. Large amounts of poisons may escape all at once. A factory fire on the River Rhine in Europe released tonnes of poisonous chemicals into the river.

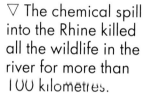

▷ A factory accident at Bhopal in India released poison gas. It damaged many people's eyesight. Many people died.

▽ The chemical spill into the Rhine killed all the wildlife in the river for more than 100 kilometres.

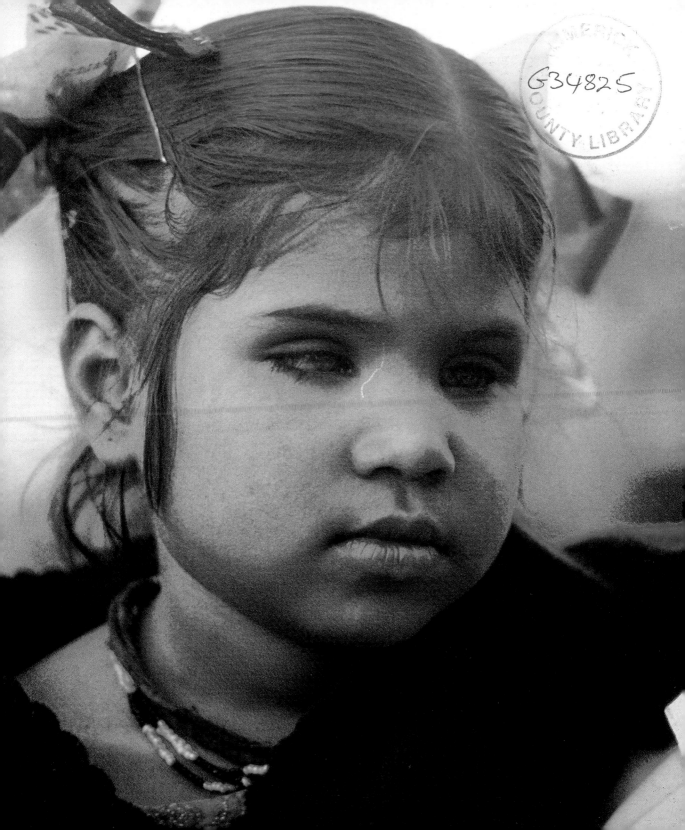

Dumps and waste

Rubbish dumps are smelly and dirty.
Rotting waste makes a home for animals
such as rats, which may spread disease.
Many factories produce rubbish which is
poisonous or catches fire easily. Dangerous
rubbish is often buried in the ground.
Over the years, the poisons may escape into
the soil and into drinking water. Most solid
waste is taken to huge **landfill sites** but we
are running out of space for
these dumps.

▷ Factories produce
millions of tonnes of
waste. Some takes
years to rot away.

◁ ▽ Rats and cockroaches live in rotting waste. They can pass diseases on to people.

▽ Waste is taken to landfill sites and covered with earth.

Why pollution continues

It is not easy to stop pollution. People need heat and light in schools, offices and homes. They want to travel in cars and aeroplanes. Everyone wants the goods that factories produce. Every year there are more people in the world to feed. It is easier and it costs less money to carry on as we are. But our world will not survive for very long with poisoned air, water and land.

▷ Nearly everyone causes pollution in everyday life.

◁ As more and more people are born, the world needs more food, factories and transport.

▷ Fertilizers can ruin
the soil but we need
big harvests to feed
the world's people.

A safer world

People all over the world are working towards a safer future. Scientists are planning new cars which will not produce harmful gases. They are testing cleaner ways of producing power, using the wind, sun and natural steam. In many countries there are new laws to stop the dumping of dangerous waste.

▽ People in many parts of the world are asking factories to stop polluting.

◁ This house uses solar energy for its heating. It has special panels which trap the heat from the sun.

▷ Wind turbines on a wind farm turn in the wind. They use the wind to produce power.

◁ In some countries, such as New Zealand, steam from inside the earth is used to produce power.

Success stories

Lakes and rivers in some countries have been cleared of rubbish and filled with fish again. There are special machines which can remove oil from the sea and there are ways of stopping oil spills from spreading. Strict laws have helped to clean up the air in busy cities like Los Angeles in the United States. But there is still much work to be done to reduce pollution as well as cleaning it up.

▷ The Thames Bubbler bubbles air into the River Thames in England. This keeps the water fresh for fish to live in.

▷ Special channels were dug to trap the oil spilled in Kuwait in 1991.

◁ Wildlife can return to rivers that have been cleaned up.

Things to do

Everyone can help to make the world a cleaner place. You can help by:

- Never dropping litter, and by joining in a local project to clean up your neighbourhood.

- Saving energy. Remember to turn off the television and the lights when they are not being used.

Useful addresses:

Friends of the Earth International
26-28 Underwood Street
London
N1 7JQ

Swedish Secretariat on Acid Rain
The Environmental Council
80 York Way
London
N1 9AG

Greenpeace
Greenpeace House
Canonbury Villas
London
N1 2BH

Glossary

acid rain Polluted rain which contains harmful acids. It poisons lakes and rivers, and is harmful to plants, animals, people and buildings.

atmosphere The layer of gases that surrounds and protects the earth. It is about 700 km thick.

fertilizers Natural or artificial plant food which is added to the soil to help crops grow.

fuels Substances which are burned to produce heat or power.

greenhouse effect The normal process by which heat is kept in the atmosphere and the earth is kept warm. Gases which trap heat in the atmosphere are known as greenhouse gases.

landfill sites Areas which have been set aside for waste to be buried in them.

pesticides Chemicals used to kill the pests and diseases which spoil crops.

pollution Wastes and other harmful substances which spoil the land, air or water

slicks Patches of oil forming a film on the surface of water.

waste Anything thrown away because it cannot be used or because it is not needed or wanted.

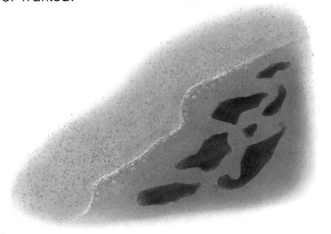

Index

Photographic credits: Mark
Edwards/Still Pictures 10; The
Environmental Picture Library
(D Cowell) 9, (E Maynard) 12;
Eye Ubiquitous (N J Hole) 23;
Chris Fairclough Colour Library
25; Frank Lane Picture Agency
(B Borrell) 15, (Silvestris) 19;
ICCE (Swersey/Liason) 3;
Panos Pictures (J Hartley) 26;
RSPB (M W Edwards) 17;
Frank Spooner Pictures
(A Purcell) 5; (Gamma) 21;
Thames Water plc 29